I0820479

WHAT I WAS MADE FOR

First published in 2026 by OH
An Imprint of HEADLINE PUBLISHING GROUP LIMITED

1

Cataloguing in Publication Data is available from the British Library

ISBN 978-1-03543-337-7

Compiled and written by Malcolm Croft
Editorial: Victoria Denne and Phoebe Hills
Designed and typeset in Avenir by Stephen Cary
Project manager: Russell Porter
Production: Arlene Lestrade
Printed and bound in Dubai

Headline's policy is to use papers that are natural, renewable and recyclable products and made from wood grown in well-managed forests and other controlled sources. The logging and manufacturing processes are expected to conform to the environmental regulations of the country of origin.

HEADLINE PUBLISHING GROUP LIMITED
An Hachette UK Company
Carmelite House, 50 Victoria Embankment, London EC4Y 0DZ

The authorised representative in the EEA is Hachette Ireland, 8 Castlecourt Centre, Dublin 15, D15 XTP3, Ireland (email: info@hbgi.ie)

www.headline.co.uk www.hachette.co.uk

WHAT I WAS MADE FOR

THE LITTLE GUIDE TO BILLIE EILISH

UNOFFICIAL AND UNAUTHORIZED

CONTENTS

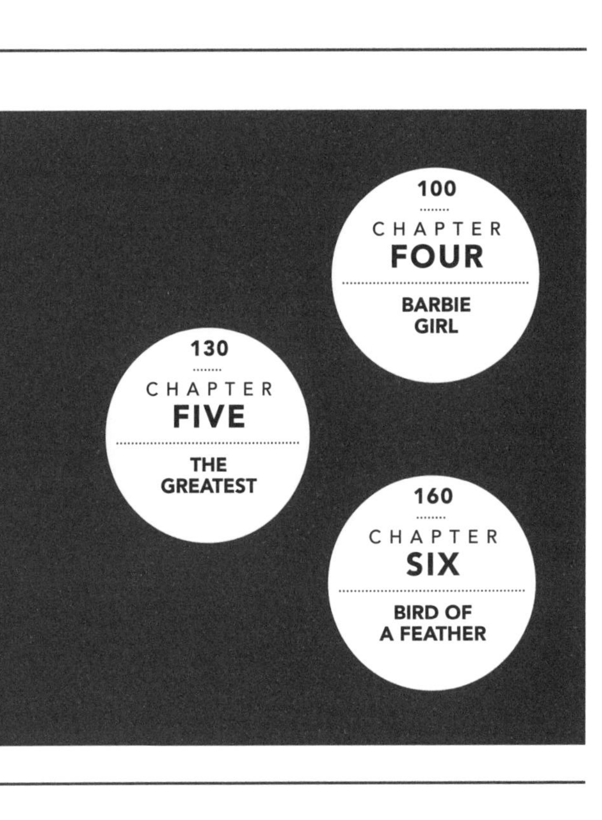
100
CHAPTER
FOUR
BARBIE GIRL
130
CHAPTER
FIVE
THE GREATEST
160
CHAPTER
SIX
BIRD OF A FEATHER

INTRODUCTION

In 2025, Billie Eilish celebrated a decade as the reigning Queen of Gen Z. Her remarkable tenure at the top has seen her collect every major accolade imaginable – Grammys, Oscars, BRITs, Golden Globes – often on multiple occasions!

Beyond the golden trophies, however, Billie's biggest claim to fame has been completely reshaping the pop landscape, for the better, forever. Her unwavering commitment to authenticity and releasing genre-defying music has profoundly influenced a generation of female artists, from Olivia Rodrigo to Charli XCX, Sabrina Carpenter to Chappell Roan, all of whom, unbelievably, are several years older than her.

Billie's worldwide fans – Pirates, as they call themselves – adore her for the no-nonsense, uncompromising approach she takes when it comes to her music and her career, as well as empowering them with a sense of confidence and power to be whomever they wish, in spite of the often harsh modern world we live in.

Put simply, Billie is the future of pop music, a saviour and anti-hero all rolled into one almighty icon who simply doesn't give a f**k. She is the pop star the world needs right now. It's what she was made for.

Inside this *Little Guide to Billie Eilish*, you'll find some of Billie's greatest words of wisdom all about herself; a thrilling mix of personal philosophies and career advice, what it feels like to be the most successful female artist in the world, and how she achieved so much so young.

At just 23 years old, Billie is only getting started. Where she goes next, of course, is anyone's guess. We can't wait.

Enjoy!

CHAPTER ONE

ORIGINAL PIRATE MATERIAL

Welcome to the weird, wild and wonder-filled world of William – sorry, Billie Eilish!

Inside, you'll discover how this totally original artist found her own way to fame, fortune and becoming everyone's favourite new singer-songwriter… and a whole lot more…

"

I was 13 when my career started – I didn't know anything. I'd go into meetings and they'd say, 'So, Billie, what do you think?' and I'd just be like, 'Am I supposed to know? Because I don't.' Eventually I got the hang of it. And now the meetings I have I explain every single detail of every single thing that I'm thinking… and people do it!

"

Billie, on being green at the beginning of her career, interview with Mark Savage, BBC, July 15, 2017.

“

All I wanted was to have a girly name, like Violet or Lavender – a pretty flowery name. I remember just being so mad at being called Billie!

”

Billie, on whether she was "proud or embarrassed of her boy-ish name", interview with British *Vogue*, May 15, 2025.

It's so weird to grow up and change in front of the world.

”

Billie, on becoming famous at age 13, interview with Lana Del Rey, *Interview* magazine, June 13, 2024.

You would never think I would enjoy wearing pretty skirts and tights, a sweater vest, being all smart and neat, but it was so cool being in choir.

Billie, on her time performing in the Los Angeles Children's Choir as a child, interview with Jonathan Heaf, *GQ* magazine, June 4, 2020.

November 18, 2015

On this day Billie uploaded "Ocean Eyes" to Soundcloud. Billie's brother Finneas originally wrote the song for his band, The Slightlys, but couldn't get it to sound the way he wanted. In October 2015, he asked Billie to sing it, realizing her voice was the perfect fit.

"It's just a beautiful song," she told *Vogue* in 2017. The track was officially released a year later, on November 18, 2016, through Darkroom and Interscope Records.

We put 'Ocean Eyes' on SoundCloud with a free download link and overnight a ton of people started sharing it. It was really surreal. Then, Danny Ruckasin, who is now my manager, reached out and was like, 'Dude, this is going to get huge. I want to help you guys.' We were like, 'That's swag!'

”

Billie, on her first taste of success, interview with Ariana Marsh, *Teen Vogue*, 24 February 2017.

My EP is called *don't smile at me* for a lot of reasons, but one of them would be when someone tells you, 'Why aren't you smiling? It's so much more beautiful when you smile.' I'm not gonna look like anybody except what I am. I want to impress myself.

”

Billie, on her debut EP *don't smile at me's* title,* interview with Rebecca Haithcoat, Ssense, 2017.

*In January 2019, *don't smile at me* became the first ever EP to reach 1 billion streams on Spotify!

My brother is my cure. Finneas makes everything better.

Billie, on her brother, Finneas, interview with British *Vogue*, May 15, 2025.

All I have ever wanted is to be on stage and have people cheering for me.

”

Billie, on performing live, interview with Jonathan Heaf, *GQ* magazine, June 4, 2020.

“There’s so many difficult parts about fame, but one of the most frustrating things is that you can’t defend or explain yourself.”

Billie, on fame – and rumours about her private life, interview with Lana Del Rey, *Interview* magazine, June 13, 2024.

I've never been to school. I grew up home-schooled, stayed home-schooled, never was not home-schooled. I still learned everything, you know? But I learned it in life.

”

Billie, on her home-schooling, YouTube interview with *Pitchfork*, November 2020.

I have a lot of internalized misogyny, and I have to say it with full transparency, I feel very grateful for being a woman right now.

Billie, on her identity as a woman, acceptance speech for *Variety*, "Billie Eilish Gives Deeply Emotional Speech", YouTube, November 17, 2023.

I almost killed myself because of Twitter a couple of years ago. Like, for real.

”

Billie, on online criticism affecting her mental health, interview with Jonathan Heaf, *GQ* magazine, June 4, 2020.

Really big fan of human rights. Really big fan of women's rights and women's reproductive rights and social justice and gun laws.

Billie, on what issues are important to her, interview with Alessandra Codinha, *Vogue*, October 8, 2024.

I always wanted to write songs just because my brother did, and also my mom did. She taught both of us how to write and so I always have high standards for writing. If I didn't, I'd have 2,000 songs!

”

Billie, on songwriting, interview with Eliza Gonzales, *Harper's Bazaar*, October 19, 2017.

My family is the most important thing in my life, so I'm with them a lot.

Billie, on her family, and taking them with her everywhere she goes, *Vanity Fair*, "Billie Eilish: The Same Interview, The Sixth Year", YouTube, November 28, 2022.

We live in a world where everyone knows everything about a song before they hear it. It doesn't even give the listener a chance to interpret it for themselves.

”

Billie, on the internet and social media affecting how music is heard these days, interview with Zane Lowe, Apple Music, May 21, 2024.

When I was four, I wrote a song about falling into a black hole. But it was really upbeat! The lyrics went 'I'm going down, down, down, into the black hole.' It went on and on!

”

Billie, on writing her first song, interview with Haley Weiss, *Interview*, February 27, 2017.

“

Finneas and I were like, ‘We made it! 1,000 listens – we’re it. That’s our whole career. We’re done.’ We thought that was a huge deal, which it was at the time, and it still is, but we thought it was because my popular friend reposted it – we didn’t think it was anything besides that. Then Hillydilly found it and Zane Lowe, and it was played on KCRW by Jason Kramer. It kind of went up from there.

”

Billie, on uploading "Ocean Eyes" in 2015 to SoundCloud, interview with Haley Weiss, *Interview* magazine, February 27, 2017.

Green and black hair felt like such a personal and career-defining look for me. It was such a magical period for me, and it was so intense. I was becoming who I am.

”

Billie, on her iconic green/black hairstyle, interview with British *Vogue*, May 15, 2025.

It was so funny to be a 14-year-old girl with my 17-year-old brother and just attending hundreds of meetings constantly with serious music industry grown-ups.

”

Billie, on becoming famous at a young age, interview with Megha Mohan and Yousef Eldin, BBC, December 6, 2022.

Happier Than Ever walked so that *Hit Me Hard and Soft* could run.

Billie, on the development of her music, interview with Zane Lowe, Apple Music, YouTube, May 21, 2024.

He was my first love and in my head he was in love with me.

”

Billie, on Justin Bieber, interview with Megha Mohan and Yousef Eldin, BBC, December 6, 2022.

“

Any person that I’m around, I’m dating.

”

Billie, in response to being asked, "What is the biggest rumour about you right now?", *Vanity Fair*, YouTube, December 18, 2024.

On March 29, 2019, Billie released her debut album, *When We All Fall Asleep, Where Do We Go?*

At just 17, she became the first artist born in the 2000s to achieve a global No. 1 album.

The album spent three weeks atop the US *Billboard* chart and remained in the Top 10 for the entire year. It sold over 7 million copies, making it by far the biggest global album of 2019, and garnered more than 6 billion Spotify streams in its first year alone.

I hated the internet having a bunch of eyes on me. I just wanted to be doing teenager shit.

”

Billie, on becoming suddenly famous at a young age, interview with Amy Kaufman, *Los Angeles Times*, July 23, 2021.

It's hard to know how to fight for what you believe in sometimes.

Billie, on the pressure of standing up for her beliefs in the public eye, interview with Jonathan Heaf, *GQ* magazine, June 4, 2020.

It's a bruising experience to grow up in the public eye, and hard to keep defending things you said as a teenager.

Billie, on things she said at age 13 coming back to haunt her, interview with Megha Mohan and Yousef Eldin, BBC, December 6, 2022.

CHAPTER TWO

DUH!

From her simple, but iconic, use of the word "Duh!" in "Bad Guy" to the grisly darkness of the words in "Birds of a Feather", Billie has never stopped being a lyrical genius.

In her words, let's now reveal even more secrets...

“

Pre-tour is just rehearsals, rehearsals, rehearsals like a motherfucker.

”

Billie, on preparing for her *Hit Me Hard and Soft* tour to ensure she gives each performance her best, interview with Alessandra Codinha, *Vogue*, October 8, 2024.

There was many, many years of me having to convince a room full of people that I knew what was right for me. I had ideas; I had plans.

”

Billie, on having enough belief in herself to control her career from the outset, interview with Arabelle Sicardi, *Allure*, September 28, 2023.

People that don't have fame have no idea how hard it is. It's fucking horrible. But you have to be respectful of people that have so much less than you and be mindful of your privilege and be polite.

Billie, on complaining about fame despite being privileged enough to have it, interview with Amy Kaufman, *Los Angeles Times*, July 23, 2021.

"

I don't feel the need to display just one version of myself.

"

Billie, on defying stereotypes because of her gender or genre, interview with Megha Mohan and Yousef Eldin, BBC, December 6, 2022.

I'm one person, I can't make any change. But the truth is, we can all make change. I have this platform and I'm going to use it.

Billie, on using her fame for positive social change, interview with Alessandra Codinha, *Vogue*, October 8, 2024.

"

It's hard enough to be a young woman not in the public eye, and just have lots of public eyes looking at you… let alone being famous and having a million people look at you constantly.

"

Billie, in reference to her 2021 song "OverHeated", and being a young successful female, interview with Lulu Garcia-Navarro, NPR, August 1, 2021.

> “I fucking hope that I’m a role model now!”

Billie, on the notion that she used to resist becoming a role model, interview with Eric Skelton, Complex, December 5, 2024.

I wish that when I was younger, I had a song like 'Your Power' to listen to.

Billie, on her 2021 single "Your Power", and its lyrical message, interview with Lulu Garcia-Navarro, NPR, August 1, 2021.

When I hear 'Your Power' I think of the man who abused his power when he was with me, how much trauma he has caused me, physically and emotionally.

”

Billie, on the traumatic real-life inspiration behind her 2021 hit single "Your Power", interview with Megha Mohan and Yousef Eldin, BBC, December 6, 2022.

If I was happy in my life, it was because people loved me on the internet. And if I was upset in my life, it was usually because people didn't.

”

Billie, on audience validation early in her career, interview with Alessandra Codinha, *Vogue*, October 8, 2024.

"Bad Guy" was the biggest global single of 2019. The song was streamed more than 2.7 billion times that year, an average of 8 million daily.

The song also garnered both Record of the Year and Song of the Year at the 62nd Grammy Awards in January 2020.

Billie revealed its inspiration to *Heat* Magazine in 2019: "'Bad Guy' is about people that are always lying about themselves. All the rappers right now are lying about how much money they have and about their house and their clothes, etc. It's like, 'Shut up, you don't have this.' It's just annoying."

I feel most powerful when I feel masculine.

Billie, on feeling powerful and wearing masculine clothing, interview with Megha Mohan and Yousef Eldin, BBC, December 6, 2022.

Finneas and I had to be very clear we weren't going to just do what anybody told us to do. People could have done crazy shit, and I didn't let them.

”

Billie, on having total control of her career, interview with Arabelle Sicardi, *Allure*, September 28, 2023.

I just was very lonely for many years. I'm not interested in that anymore.

Billie, on remaining single for the first few years of her early fame, interview with Alessandra Codinha, *Vogue*, October 8, 2024.

I literally hate who I am so much when I'm in love. I don't like being vulnerable in a romantic way. It makes me feel uncomfortable.

Billie, on "the dangers of falling in love", interview with Lana Del Rey, *Interview* magazine, June 13, 2024.

“

You don’t have to be exceptional. You can just be a person and get awards for just being. Women should know.

”

Billie, on the industry pressure to always look and behave a certain way, interview with Arabelle Sicardi, *Allure*, September 28, 2023.

It's impossible to describe to other people what it's like to be so famous. It's like trying to explain a colour that doesn't exist.

Billie, on being famous, interview with Megha Mohan and Yousef Eldin, BBC, December 6, 2022.

Diagnosed in childhood, Billie's Tourette's manifests as involuntary tics, primarily eye-bulging and head-twitching, often triggered by stress. She joins a list of famous neurodivergent individuals who have Tourette's, including Kurt Cobain and Lewis Capaldi.

The condition has its positives: strong verbal skills, tenacity, creativity, empathy, and hyperfocus. Eilish publicly revealed her diagnosis on *The Ellen Show* in April 2019, telling Ellen DeGeneres, "A lot of my fans have Tourette's, which made me feel kind of more at home with saying it, and also I felt like there was a connection there."

The love of my life is singing. And I didn't realize that you can train that instrument and have even more fun with it. It's fucking *awesome* to learn.

Billie, on "studying the art of singing", interview with Alessandra Codinha, *Vogue*, October 8, 2024.

I don't ever feel like I'm above anyone when I'm on stage: I feel like one with them, and I feel like I want to impress them and just have fun with them.

Billie, on performing *with* her fans (not just *for* them), interview with Lulu Garcia-Navarro, NPR, August 1, 2021.

Being a woman is just such a war, forever. Especially being a young woman in the public eye. It's really unfair.

”

Billie, on being a female pop star, interview with Katcy Stephan, *Variety*, November 13, 2023.

I feel best right out of the shower, with my lotions and my smells.

Billie, on how she makes herself feel good when feeling "overexposed", interview with Arabelle Sicardi, *Allure*, September 28, 2023.

"

It turns out that I'm young – I have a whole life of cool shit I can do.

"

Billie, on the benefits of having to mature fast in the music industry at a young age, interview with Katcy Stephan, *Variety*, November 13, 2023.

I've had such a good relationship with the fans since the beginning, and they have literally been the number-one priority for me.

Billie, on the inspiration she receives from her loyal fans, interview with Miranda Sawyer, *The Irish Times*, August 3, 2021.

Hit Me Hard and Soft is the best thing Finneas and I have ever made. And that's why it was so punishing to make.

”

Billie, on her third studio album, released in 2024, YouTube, December 18, 2024.

Finneas and I look at each other in silence and we both know we're thinking the same exact thing.

”

Billie, on being able to "read Finneas's mind", interview with British *Vogue*, May 15, 2025.

I would love to be a hot girl.

Billie, on her looks, and referencing jazz singer Julie London, interview with Amy Kaufman, *Los Angeles Times*, July 23, 2021.

I am undeniably who I am, and I have absolutely no other choice, and sometimes it feels like a burden – but I happen to also like that girl.

Billie, on finally having confidence in her identity, interview with British *Vogue*, May 15, 2025.

CHAPTER THREE

HAPPIER THAN EVER

As Billie's fame grew so did her sense of self, transforming from an overwhelmed teenager in baggy clothes into a strong, independent young woman, completely confident in her own skin.

Today, Billie 2.0 is happier than ever…

“

Any time I’m creating anything, I’m thinking about the video, I’m thinking about the artwork and I’m thinking about the colours. Everything that I make, I’m already thinking of what colour it is, what texture it is.

”

Billie, on her synesthesia, interview with Josh Eells, *Rolling Stone*, July 31, 2019.

Beyond Tourette's, ADHD and night terrors, Billie also experiences synesthesia, a neurological condition where senses blend. For her, music evokes specific shapes, smells and colours.

This heightened sensory perception is crucial to Billie's songwriting, enabling her to visualize sounds. For instance, "Bad Guy" appears as yellow, the number seven, and "smells like cookies".

This rare condition, affecting roughly one in 25,000 people in the US, is also shared by other notable artists such as Pharrell Williams, Chris Martin, Marina Diamandis… and Finneas!

I've made enough people feel good that I deserve to feel good too.

”

Billie, on deserving to be herself all the time, interview with Arabelle Sicardi, *Allure*, September 28, 2023.

I didn't want people to have access to my body, even visually.

”

Billie, on her clothing choices in her early career, interview with Katcy Stephan, *Variety*, November 13, 2023.

I'm outspoken in my own way. I really don't like shoving information down people's throats.

Billie, on (politely) educating her audience on current issues, interview with Katcy Stephan, *Variety*, November 13, 2023.

Even though I come off as very open and bold, I don't tell the internet shit about my actual life.

Billie, on keeping personal secrets offline, interview with Amy Kaufman, *Los Angeles Times*, July 23, 2021.

The more I think about being myself, the better my life is. The more I am myself, the better my life is.

”

Billie, on being herself, interview with Arabelle Sicardi, *Allure*, September 28, 2023.

“

It’s always scary when you fall in love, it’s hard to know what the hell is going on because you’re blinded by this curtain of lust and love and admiration.

”

Billie, on protecting herself from being hurt, *Vanity Fair*, YouTube, December 18, 2024.

I didn't know I was coming out, but I kinda thought, wasn't it obvious? I didn't realize people didn't know. I've been doing this for a long time, and I just didn't talk about it. Whoops. I saw the article, and I was like, 'Oh, I guess I came out today!' It's exciting to me because I guess people didn't know, so it's cool that they know… I am for the girls.

”

Billie, on coming out in an interview with *Vanity Fair*, interview with *Vanity Fair*, YouTube, December 18, 2024.

“

I felt like my body was gaslighting me for years. I had to go through a process of being like, ‘My body is actually me’. And it’s not out to get me.

”

Billie, on her hip injury and hypermobility, interview with Jen Wang, *Vogue*, January 4, 2023.

I think my purpose is to share my fucking art so people can connect to it.

”

Billie, on her purpose, interview with Eric Skelton, *Complex*, December 5, 2024.

"I've never felt like a woman. I've never felt desirable. I've never felt feminine."

Billie, on having previous relationships and partners who never made her feel desired, interview with Katcy Stephan, *Variety*, November 13, 2023.

I just feel so connected to my fans because we were all the same age when I became famous... we grew up together and that was hugely comforting to me.

”

Billie, on becoming famous as a teenager and having teenage fans, interview with Terry Gross, NPR, December 17, 2024.

I was so unhappy and so joyless, I genuinely didn't think I'd make it to 17. I don't want to be too dark, but I think about this one time I was in Berlin and I was alone in my hotel… And I remember there was a window right there… I remember crying because I was thinking about how the way that I was going to die was... I was going to do it.

Billie, on her fragile state of mind when she was 17, interview with Gayle King, CBS News, January 24, 2020.

Billie's made many famous friends over the years. This is what they have to say about just how great she is!

"I think that it's the closest I am with Billie to like total trust of anyone. And total vulnerability."

Finneas O'Connell,
CBS News, January 10, 2024.

"Billie is doing her own thing. Nobody's telling her what to do."

Thom Yorke,
sourced from iHeart.com, July 31, 2019.

"When I heard 'Everything I Wanted' I just sobbed."

Selena Gomez,
interview with Zane Lowe, sourced from YouTube.

"Everything Billie does is just beautiful."

Sam Smith,
sourced from YouTube.

"Billie Eilish is just the best thing to happen to the music industry in a long time."

Niall Horan,
interview with Capital FM, sourced from YouTube.

"From the moment I heard her voice I knew she was going to be a star."

Khalid,
interview with Ellen, sourced from YouTube.

"Billie's really just showing people how it looks to be comfortable being yourself."

Alicia Keys,
interview with *Entertainment Tonight*

I'm not going to let somebody take away my sparkle, as they say.

”

Billie, on past relationships that ended negatively, *Vanity Fair*, YouTube, December 18, 2024.

"I just want to be making the difference and shutting the fuck up about it."

Billie, on keeping her activism private, interview with Jen Wang, *Vogue*, January 4, 2023.

My favourite singers are all kind of old jazz singers that I've always looked up to. They're all wearing tight, corseted dresses with their hair done. Thank God that those women came before me 'cause otherwise, I wouldn't have been able to do anything.

Billie, on whether she was influenced by the men in hip-hop in terms of dress as opposed to the women, interview with Terry Gross, NPR, December 17, 2024.

"

I don't want my kids to be a famous person's kids. I hate famous people's kids – they are so bratty!

"

Billie, on kids and starting her own family, interview with Jonathan Heaf, *GQ* magazine, June 4, 2020.

Wow, wow, wow, wow, wow, wow. Oh my God. I'm sorry. Thank you so much. This is my first Grammy's. I never thought this would ever happen in my whole life!

”

On January 26, 2020, Billie dominated the Grammy Awards. She won five out of her six nominations, including all four of the night's most coveted categories: Best New Artist, Record of the Year, Song of the Year and Album of the Year.

The iconic photograph of her struggling to hold all her awards quickly went viral. Billie's triumph also made her the first woman and the youngest person ever to win these four main Grammy categories.

Billie's full legal name is Billie Eilish Pirate Baird O'Connell; she was named Billie in honour of her grandfather, Bill, who passed away just before her birth.

The name "Pirate" came from her older brother, Finneas, who, at age four, affectionately called her "Pirate" during their mother's pregnancy due to his love for pirates.

While embracing her "Pirate" side, Billie has publicly expressed her dislike for her legal last name, O'Connell, jokingly telling *Rolling Stone* in 2019 that it "sounds like if a goat was a person – Billie Goat O'Connell!"

I wish no one knew anything about my sexuality or anything about my dating life. Ever, ever, *ever*.

Billie, on discussing her private life in public, interview with Alessandra Codinha, *Vogue*, October 8, 2024.

I have never felt powerful in a relationship. I did once and, guess what, I took advantage of that person's kindness. I wasn't used to it.

Billie, on the complexities of her relationships, interview with Jonathan Heaf, *GQ* magazine, June 4, 2020.

The undisputed
Queen of Gen-Z Pop,
Billie has, so far,
sold more than
11 million albums
and 46 million digital
singles!

I've never been dumped. I've never been broken up with. I've only done the breaking up.

”

Billie, on relationships, interview with Lana Del Rey, *Interview* magazine, June 13, 2024.

"My body is mine and yours is yours. Our own bodies are kind of the only real things which are truly ours. I get to see it and get to show it – when I want to."

Billie, on bodily autonomy, interview with Jonathan Heaf, *GQ* magazine, June 4, 2020.

I'm the type of person if you tell me to stop doing something, I'm going to do the opposite.

"

Billie, on having attitude, interview with Thomas Smith, NME.com, January 4, 2019.

I wish I could just save the world alone. Grow my own food and live off the grid. Erase my carbon footprint.

Billie, on being young and environmentally conscious, interview with Jen Wang, *Vogue*, January 4, 2023.

I have a really big problem with control.

”

Billie, on having total control of her career and private life, interview with Arabelle Sicardi, *Allure*, September 28, 2023.

CHAPTER FOUR

BARBIE GIRL

Billie is no Barbie Girl, and yet, paradoxically, she's the perfect fit.

From baggy clothes, to blending in, to believing in herself, Billie's rise to Gen Z role model is precisely what she was made for...

The way that 'What Was I Made For?' has been heard and seen by women is so special to me.

”

Billie, on her 2023 single "What Was I Made For?", interview with Arabelle Sicardi, *Allure*, September 28, 2023.

The hard thing about directing, especially when you're not super experienced, is that you have this vision, but you don't necessarily know how to achieve it. I directed the video for 'What Was I Made For?' and it's one of my favourite things I've ever made.

99

Billie, on directing her own music videos, interview with *Vanity Fair*, December 7, 2023.

"I've been dreaming of all this since I was little. I don't want to take anything for granted. That's my one wish."

Billie, on getting everything she wanted, interview with Ed Power, *Hot Press*, February 18, 2018.

I'm so lucky that my art has given me the opportunity to use my platform for things I truly care about. There are so many ways artists can use their platforms in a non-preachy, self-serving way, and I really do try to use mine as much as possible, because what's the point otherwise?

Billie, on "using her art as a form of environmental activism", interview with British *Vogue*, May 15, 2025.

"

We wrote most of 'What Was I Made For?' without thinking about ourselves and our own lives but thinking about this character we were inspired by. A couple of days went by, and I realized it was about me. It's everything I feel. And it's not just me – everyone feels like that, eventually.

"

Billie, on writing her 2023 single "What Was I Made For?", interview with Arabelle Sicardi, *Allure*, September 28, 2023.

My biggest love language is physical touch. I just need to be touching skin, all the time.

Billie, on what makes her happy in a relationship, *Vanity Fair*, "Billie Eilish: The Same Interview, The Sixth Year", YouTube, November 28, 2022.

I've settled for less than I deserved, and I'm not going to do that anymore.

”

Billie, on getting what she feels she deserves, interview with Arabelle Sicardi, *Allure*, September 28, 2023.

"

I think life is always about going back to who you originally were. The older I get, the more I'm doing things I enjoyed when I was a kid and being who I was when I was a kid.

"

Billie, on reclaiming some of her lost childhood, interview with Eric Skelton, Complex, December 5, 2024.

Being loved and loving is the greatest gift in life. It's worth getting hurt for.

Billie, on what her closest friendships have taught her, interview with British *Vogue*, May 15, 2025.

“

I don’t like being high-maintenance. I don’t like showing pain. I don’t cry. *Ever.*

Billie, on vulnerability, interview with Eve Barlow, *Elle*, September 5, 2019.

Billie has earned 18 Guinness World Records...

- Youngest female artist at No.1 on UK albums chart
- Most simultaneous US Hot 100 entries by a female
- Most streams on Spotify in one year (female)
- Youngest Album of the Year winner at the Grammy Awards
- Youngest artist to win all four Grammy Awards general field categories
- Youngest Record of the Year winner at the Grammys
- Youngest solo artist to win Album of the Year at the Grammys
- First female artist to win all four Grammys
- Youngest musician to write and record a James Bond theme song
- Most consecutive Record of the Year awards won at the Grammys

- Most viewed Wikipedia page for a 'post-millennial'
- Most pre-added album on Apple Music
- Most consecutive Grammy nominations for Record of the Year (female)
- Most consecutive Grammy nominations for Song of the Year
- Youngest winner of Best International Artist of the Year at the BRIT Awards
- Youngest person to win the film music awards "triple crown"
- First songwriter in history to receive an award at the Palm Springs International Film Festival
- Most Grammys won for Song of the Year ("Birds of a Feather")

If I was a guy and I was wearing these baggy clothes, nobody would bat an eye. There's people out there saying, 'Dress like a girl for once! Wear tight clothes you'd be much prettier and your career would be so much better!' No it wouldn't. It literally would not.

”

Billie, on her baggy clothes, interview with Patrick Clarke, *NME*, January 10, 2019.

"I gotta find stuff within myself and my personal life that has nothing to do with the outside world or the internet or my status that's going to bring me that much joy."

Billie, on finding passions outside of music and fame, interview with Katcy Stephan, *Variety*, November 13, 2023.

I felt the need to change it all the time when I was more unstable.

Billie, on dying her hair, interview with Amy Kaufman, *Los Angeles Times*, July 23, 2021.

“

I feel like I helped bring people together, and it felt so special. I wasn't expecting to have women around the world feel connected.

Billie, on the audience response to her 2023 single "What Was I Made For?", interview with Katcy Stephan, *Variety*, November 13, 2023.

Nobody understands: my music is actually a job. Just because I'm 16 and it isn't boring doesn't mean it's not a job – it doesn't mean I'm not working every day, really hard, for something I want.

”

Billie, on working hard at her music and not being able to spend time with her friends, interview with Ed Power, *Hot Press*, February 18, 2018.

In March 2024, Billie achieved the rare "triple crown" of entertainment awards, winning an Oscar, Grammy and Golden Globe for "What Was I Made For?" from the Barbie soundtrack.

Upon receiving the final accolade at the Academy Awards on March 10, 2024, Billie told the audience how overwhelming the thought of winning an Oscar was: "I had a nightmare about this last night!"

> “I wasn’t trying to create ‘my brand’ or trying to break the rules. I wasn’t doing something to make kids like me. I just literally did what I wanted. That’s the only reason it worked.”

Billie, on making music true to herself without compromise, interview with Decca Aitkenhead, *Hey Mag*, September 29, 2019.

It's really important that young women know that being taken advantage of can happen to anyone.

Billie, on her 2021 single "Your Power", interview with Amy Kaufman, *Los Angeles Times*, July 23, 2021.

Kids know more than adults.

”

Billie, on connecting to her fans as a teenager, interview with Eve Barlow, *Elle*, September 5, 2019.

> “When I’m on stage I have to disassociate from the ideas I have of my body.”

Billie, on her “physical wildness” on stage, interview with Miranda Sawyer, *Irish Times*, August 3, 2021.

It was as if 'What Was I Made For' was a tiny creature inside of me for years, scratching the inside of me.

”

Billie, on writing and recording "What Was I Made For", interview with Arabelle Sicardi, *Allure*, September 28, 2023.

My family is like everybody's. There's anger – and love, so it kind of evens out.

Billie, on what causes her stress, interview with Miranda Sawyer, *Irish Times*, August 3, 2021.

With songwriting, you have to give yourself permission to write a bad song.

Billie, on songwriting, interview with Terry Gross, NPR, December 17, 2024.

When I think too much about how I can never have privacy again, it's enough to make me want to do all sorts of crazy things.

”

Billie, on her lack of privacy and wanting to act out as a result, interview with Arabelle Sicardi, *Allure*, September 28, 2023.

I used to read every single comment and every picture I was tagged in and respond to every single DM, but now I can't go on Instagram. I can't handle that shit.

Billie, on social media, interview with Patrick Clarke, *NME*, January 10, 2019.

In an interview with Australian radio station Triple J, Billie revealed her "strange addiction" to the American sitcom *The Office*, which directly inspired her song "My Strange Addiction".

She explained, "I've seen *The Office* 12 times now and counting. Every time I finish it, I start it immediately right after from the beginning again. I have episodes memorized, it's my therapy, my little escape. As stupid as that sounds, that show has gotten me through my whole life."

CHAPTER FIVE

THE GREATEST

There is no one on Earth quite like Billie Eilish. She defies and then defines all genres and categories she's put in, both musically and culturally.

Put simply: she's the greatest spokesperson for her generation – as these words of her wisdom attest…

On June 24, 2022, Billie's performance at the world's largest and most iconic festival, Glastonbury, became a pivotal moment in her career – and the festival's history.

At just 20 years old, she became the youngest solo headliner in the festival's five-decade existence. Her 20-song set drew over 100,000 revellers, marking one of the largest attendances ever recorded.

I'm not a category of a person. I'm a person. The same person, for the whole of my life.

99

Billie, on the relationship between aesthetics and music, interview with Lulu Garcia-Navarro, NPR, August 1, 2021.

I would rather suffer in silence than tell you something's bothering me and have you think I'm sensitive.

Billie, on trying hard to not express her emotions, interview with Lana Del Rey, *Interview* magazine, June 13, 2024.

In the beginning there were all these radio people that wouldn't play me because I was 'too sad' and 'no one was going to relate to it.'

”

Billie, on early negativity to her music, interview with Gayle King, *CBS News Sunday Morning*, YouTube, January 24, 2020.

I've always been afraid of being bad at something because when you're a girl and you're bad at something, once, then all the boys think you're bad at that forever.

Billie, on feeling pressured as a woman to constantly be flawless, interview with Anthony Mason, *CBS News Sunday Morning*, YouTube, December 10, 2024.

I had moments of thinking, 'Oh, my God, "Birds of a Feather" is our worst song,' I thought it was too poppy and that everyone was gonna hate it.

Billie, on "trying new things" on her album *Hit Me Hard and Soft*, in conversation with Mikael Wood, *Los Angeles Times*, October 10, 2024.

I was wearing all these baggy clothes, and it was my style, but at the same time, it was how I could feel comfortable in my body and not feel tied to how my body looks. I didn't want my body to be part of my outfit. I wanted my outfit to be my outfit, and my body happens to be inside it.

Billie, on her "baggy clothes" era, interview with Eric Skelton, Complex, December 5, 2024.

I'm so much more interested in being like other girls because other girls are fuckin' tight. I love women!

”

Billie, on "not feeling like a woman", acceptance speech for *Variety*, "Billie Eilish Gives Deeply Emotional Speech", YouTube, November 17, 2023.

"

Pressure is not something you can see, it's just there. There is pressure on me. But I don't feel debilitated by it, I don't feel controlled by it.

"

Billie, on feeling pressured as a young woman in the music industry, *Vanity Fair,* "Billie Eilish: The Same Interview, The Sixth Year", YouTube, November 28, 2022.

"

It's really important to promote happiness, and loving yourself and stuff, but a lot of people don't love themselves. Everybody feels sadness in their lives.

"

Billie, on the darker themes of her music,
interview with Gayle King, *CBS News Sunday Morning*,
YouTube, January 24, 2020.

> “
> I never said, ‘Fuck pop!’ I just made the music I wanted to make.
> ”

Billie, on the media’s “rebel” narrative about her “sadcore pop” music, interview with Eve Barlow, *Elle*, September 5, 2019.

I feel better about myself than I ever have. Which makes me feel proud, I worked really hard on it.

Billie, reflecting on her past year and her hopes for 2023, *Vanity Fair*, "Billie Eilish: The Same Interview, The Sixth Year", YouTube, November 28, 2022.

I would rather not do a show than do a mediocre version. I am one thousand percent serious.

”

Billie, on performing with an injury, interview with Eve Barlow, *Elle*, September 5, 2019.

I wore a tank top once and suddenly my boobs are trending on Twitter. Which is fine – that shit looks good.

Billie, on her boobs going viral, interview with Jonathan Heaf, *GQ* magazine, June 4, 2020.

My adrenaline's like Hulk, dude.

”

Billie, on how she feels before a live show, interview with Eve Barlow, *Elle*, September 5, 2019.

A lot of moments on *Hit Me Hard and Soft* are about situations where I was like, 'I'd rather be tortured inside but have somebody think that I'm cool, than have somebody think that I'm hysterical and actually express my feelings.' I come off as a person that doesn't care.

”

Billie, on the darker themes of her music,
interview with Gayle King, *CBS News Sunday Morning*,
YouTube, January 24, 2020.

I remember everything about who I was, but I don't recognize that person anymore. When I turned 16, I died, and I got reincarnated as Billie Eilish.

”

Billie, on her internal world changing with her external reality, interview with Decca Aitkenhead, *Hey Mag*, September 29, 2019.

I've had to really convince myself that I am beautiful. Being a woman is hard.

”

Billie, on feeling beautiful in spite of how she often feels, interview with British *Vogue*, May 15, 2025.

I would watch videos of different male performers on stage and just feel this deep sadness in my body that I'll never be able to take my shirt off on stage and run around.

”

Billie, on feeling envious of male performers, interview with Terry Gross, NPR, December 17, 2024.

It's worth it because it lets me play shows and meet people, but fame itself is fuckin' dreadful.

”

Billie, interview with Cady Drell, *Marie Claire*, 7 February 2019.

I tried to be like everyone else. I tried to fit in. But it made me miserable, and it also made me annoying, because it wasn't authentic.

Billie, on being different and "never doubting her creative judgement", interview with Decca Aitkenhead, *Hey Mag*, September 29, 2019.

I have to give credit to the person I've always been – I did not give a fuck at all.

Billie, on remaining consistent in who she is, interview with Arabelle Sicardi, *Allure*, September 28, 2023.

More praise from Billie's most famous admirers...

"We must protect Billie, beings like her don't enter our orbit often."

Katy Perry,
@katyperry, Instagram, April 15, 2019.

"People say, 'Is rock dead?' When I look at someone like Billie Eilish, rock and roll is not close to dead."

Dave Grohl,
sourced from TheThings.com, April 4, 2020.

"She's the voice of our generation."

Lana Del Rey,
News.com.au, April 14, 2024.

"Talent like hers doesn't come along very often."

Elton John,
sourced from TheThings.com, April 4, 2020.

"Billie Eilish is everything. She's a little heavenly creature for sure that one."

Julia Roberts,
Refinery29, December 7, 2018.

"You've saved the movies, last summer. All of our jobs. You've delivered joy to countless generations and genders of people, and you should surf that wave, kids – until you are old and deserve to be jaded like me."

Meryl Streep,
People magazine, January 5, 2024

I have impending-doom feelings most of the day.

”

Billie, on her daily confrontations with her mental health, interview with Arabelle Sicardi, *Allure*, September 28, 2023.

"I really don't like to be alone. I have a lot of stalkers, and I have people that want to do bad things to me, and I also am freaked out by the dark and, like, what's under beds and couches."

Billie, on what scares her the most, interview with Miranda Sawyer, *Irish Times*, August 3, 2021.

Everyone's allowed to do and eat whatever they want. But the misconception that it isn't completely, unreasonably inhumane to abuse and slaughter animals just for the pleasure of something that tastes good is silly and thoughtless to me.

Billie, on her veganism, interview with British *Vogue*, May 15, 2025.

I'm so intimidated by women and their beauty and their presence.

Billie, on being attracted to women, interview with Katcy Stephan, *Variety*, November 13, 2023.

CHAPTER SIX

BIRDS OF A FEATHER

To her fans, her Pirates, Billie is their designated bird of a feather, the artist that best represents their shared beliefs, be it politics, music, identity or sexuality.

For one last time, let us bask in Billie's brilliant wit and wisdom on these subjects – and beyond!

We're really close. We go through a lot of the same things even though we're five years apart. He sings and he writes a ton, and I write a ton, and we write together. He does tons of harmonies, and we always perform together. We're a team.

”

Billie, on working with her brother Finneas, interview with Haley Weiss, *Interview* magazine, February 27, 2017.

My dad used to make us mixtapes of all the stuff that he liked, which was Avril Lavigne, Linkin Park, Green Day, and a ton of the Beatles – the Beatles was a huge thing growing up.

”

Billie, on her earliest influences, interview with Haley Weiss, *Interview* magazine, February 27, 2017.

I've always been a music listener. It's crazy to me that people only find music by going to the most popular hits. What the fuck are you doing?

”

Billie, on discovering new music, interview with Eve Barlow, *Elle*, September 5, 2019.

I just love the idea of glorifying people's biggest fears. I just really wanted something that's going to kind of make you jump a little bit.

Billie, on the intensity of her music videos, interview with Michel Martin and Gemma Watters, NPR, March 27, 2019.

When you're younger, you try out different personalities because you don't know which one is you, to be honest.

Billie, on her trial-and-error approach to discovering who she is, interview with Michel Martin and Gemma Watters, NPR, March 27, 2019.

If somebody said something to me in person, I'd beat their ass.

Billie, on meeting her online trolls in real life, interview with Patrick Clarke, *NME*, January 10, 2019.

“There’s a lot of lying going on on the internet. The whole internet is very gullible because all it wants to hear is drama.”

Billie, on social media and the internet,
interview with Michel Martin and Gemma Watters, NPR,
March 27, 2019.

I went through a week of thinking smoking would be cool, but then… no. My lungs are beautiful. Fucking beautiful, dog.

”

Billie, on experimenting with new experiences as a teenager, interview with Jonathan Heaf, *GQ* magazine, June 4, 2020.

“

Whenever I sing ‘Oxytocin’ on stage, I have to think about sex. I have no problem with that.

”

Billie, on using her synesthesia and imagination for songwriting, interview with Miranda Sawyer, *Irish Times*, August 3, 2021.

People are like, 'Oh, Billie Eilish, she said this and now she says this.' I'm like, bro! I was 13 when all this started. What do you expect from a 15-year-old's mouth? To not say a bunch of dumb shit?

Billie, on things she regrets she said when she first started, interview with Jonathan Heaf, *GQ* magazine, June 4, 2020.

If I wasn't doing this I would be miserable because this is always what I've wanted.

”

Billie, on making her dreams come true, interview with Patrick Clarke, *NME*, January 10, 2019.

I have never done drugs, I've never got high, I've never smoked anything in my life. I don't give a fuck, I never have. It's just not interesting to me. I have other shit to do.

”

Billie, on drugs, interview with Hannah Ewens, *The Guardian*, March 29, 2019.

At just 18 years old, Billie Eilish was tapped by James Bond producers to write and perform the theme for 2021's *No Time To Die*. This made her the youngest singer to record a Bond theme.

The song not only earned Billie and Finneas their first Academy Award for "Best Original Song" in February 2022, making Billie the first person born in the 21st century to win an Oscar, but it also marked the third consecutive Bond theme to win the award, following Adele's "Skyfall" and Sam Smith's "Writing on the Wall".

I really wanted to be a model when I was little. I loved photography and I loved being on camera. But I was short and chubby so I couldn't. Being an artist is way more interesting than just being a model because it's about you and what you want to be. You're not being treated likea clothes hanger.

”

Billie, on her earliest career aspirations, interview with David Smyth, *Evening Standard*, October 30, 2017.

I'm obsessed with the idea of nonchalance.

Billie, on not giving a fuck, interview with Lana Del Rey, *Interview* magazine, June 13, 2024.

“

It makes me sick to my stomach thinking about if I had to be around the younger Billie, it really freaks me out sometimes. She was a scary girl.

”

Billie, on what she was like as a teenager, interview with Conan O'Brien, Team Coco, "Billie Eilish Was An Intimidating Teenager", YouTube, March 29, 2023.

I've never really felt like I could relate to girls very well. But I love them so much.

Billie, on being a "girl's girl", interview with Katcy Stephan, *Variety*, November 13, 2023.

I want to make people realize things that they didn't even know that they knew. I want to say things that get to people in a way other things can't, because knowing how you feel but not knowing why you feel that way can be really, really hard. If there is a song that just says exactly how you feel, I think that is really important.

Billie, on making her fans feel things through her music, interview with *Coup de Main*, January 23, 2017.

I'm never gonna be 27 – that's too old.

”

Billie, on growing older, interview with Josh Eells, *Rolling Stone*, 31 July 2019.

I had no idea when I was younger that I was doing anything fearlessly. When I would hear people comment that I was only 16 and not fitting in with the stereotype – that I was a rebel or whatever – I remember being really confused because I didn't see it that way. I just felt like I was doing what I thought was cool. I was not intentionally trying to break any mould or rules or change music. I kind of just stayed true to what I liked and what I wanted.

Billie, on being fearless, interview with British *Vogue*, May 15, 2025.

I love singing more than anything in the world. And it was really nice on *Hit Me Hard and Soft* to let myself sing how my soul wanted to.

”

Billie, in response to being asked about "leaning into different vocal textures and flexing vocal ability" in her album *Hit Me Hard and Soft*, interview with *British Vogue*, May 15, 2025.

Dopamine! I love activities. I love doing stuff. I can't be stagnant. That's what really makes me happy, things that make me feel activated and stimulated and alive. So… anything that involves dopamine.

Billie, when asked "What makes her the happiest?", interview with British *Vogue*, May 15, 2025.

I know the ins and outs of this industry, and what people actually use in photos, and I actually know what looks real can be fake.

”

Billie, on social media appearance, interview with Miranda Sawyer, *Irish Times,* August 3, 2021.

Charli XCX and I got on the phone and talked about which song I could feature on. 'Guess' was my favourite song from her album, and oh my God, I was so excited. We made it in under a week, including the video, and then it came out like three days later. It was awesome.

”

Billie, on collaborating with Charli XCX and featuring on her song "Guess" from *Brat and It's Completely Different but Also Still Brat*, interview with Eric Skelton, Complex, December 5, 2024.

Sometimes I dress like a boy. Sometimes I dress like a swaggy girl. And sometimes I feel trapped by this persona that I have created, because sometimes I think people view me not as a woman.

Billie, on her style and avoiding being sexualized, interview with Jonathan Heaf, *GQ* magazine, June 4, 2020.

Blending in, I have never understood that at all. Why would you want to be in a room of people that look exactly like you? I don't know. What's the point of dressing like someone else? They're already dressing that way. Do your own stuff. I've always known what I want and who I wanted to be, what I wanted to wear and who I wanted to be seen as.

Billie, on being and looking like herself, interview with Rebecca Haithcoat, Ssense, 28 February 2018.

“

We only need bodies to eat and walk around and poop. We only need them to survive. It’s ridiculous that anybody even cares about bodies at all. Like, why? Why do we care?

”

Billie, on public perception of her body, interview with Miranda Sawyer, *Irish Times*, August 3, 2021.

I would love to feel safe as a woman in my country.

Billie, endorsing Kamala Harris for President of the USA, and not feeling safe as a woman in America, interview with Alessandra Codinha, *Vogue*, October 8, 2024.

Nobody that knows me thinks I'm a dark person. I'm always laughing… at everything.

”

Billie, on the darker themes of her music, interview with Gayle King, *CBS News Sunday Morning*, YouTube, January 24, 2020.

I just feel so connected to my fans because we were all the same age when I became famous… we grew up together and that was hugely comforting to me.

”

Billie, on becoming famous as a teenager and having teenage fans, interview with Terry Gross, NPR, December 17, 2024.

When you get to a certain level of fame or notoriety, it doesn't matter what you say or do, you are a certain level of known. You will be super hated. And super loved.

Billie, on her (then) newfound fame, interview with Jonathan Heaf, *GQ* magazine, June 4, 2020.